The Pain Tree

and Other Teenage Angst-Ridden Poetry

collected and illustrated by

Esther Pearl Watson *and* **Mark Todd**

Houghton Mifflin Company
Boston 2000

We would like to thank all the teens who so generously contributed their poems for this book.
We would also like to acknowledge Seventeen and react magazine,
an Advance Magazine Publication, for their efforts.

CONTENTS

WORDS FROM THE ARTISTS

THE POETRY I WROTE WHEN I was a teenager was dramatic and full of raw emotion. I wanted to tell the world all about my problems; I needed to be heard. My poetry was filled with pain and anguish, but in reality, my teen life wasn't terribly traumatic; in fact, it was quite ordinary. Once, I wrote about an abusive stepfather I didn't have, prompting the concern of my tenth-grade teacher. "I'm worried about you; let's talk about this," she scrawled at the bottom of my paper. On other occasions I wrote about war and death, things I knew nothing about. I tried to write what I thought people wanted to hear. In retrospect, it seems that my poetry wasn't really about me at all. I soon discovered that I could be emotionally more honest through a different mode of expression, drawing and painting.

This book started out as a personal project. As an artist I'm always looking for unusual ways to promote my work, and teen poetry, with its dreamlike visuals and intense emotions, seemed a perfect match for my illustrations. I approached friends, asking them if they had kept any of their old writing hidden away. It took some convincing to get them to share these private and often embarrassingly painful teenage memories. I illustrated each poem and printed and bound five hundred 'zines.

When Esther and I decided to turn this 'zine into a book, we needed more poems, and we wanted to hear other teen voices from around the country. So we searched teen Web sites and got help from the editors of **re**act and *Seventeen* magazines. After we had collected twenty-five poems, I took on the boys' illustrations while Esther tackled the girls'. *The Pain Tree* has grown from a black-and-white 'zine into a colorful showcase of poetic teenage gems.

—MARK TODD

DURING MY SEARCH FOR TEEN POETS ON THE Internet, I was amazed by how many young people dedicated their Web sites to poetry. As I scrolled through endless sites, I began to wonder whether kids still kept poetry in spiral-bound notebooks, written with funky purple ink, hidden away from little brothers and nosy moms.

I've kept a daily journal since the age of thirteen. Mostly I write about how I feel each day. As a teenager I carried my journals around everywhere I went. There was a time during my high school years when my emotions were so strong and confusing that it was difficult to put my feelings into words. My parents were getting divorced, and I was working two jobs after school to try to save enough money to move to California so I could go to college. Free-verse poetry gave me the freedom to write whatever came to mind. There were no rules to follow, and my poetry didn't always make sense. Writing helped me sort things out and got me through tough times. I could let off some steam or just kick around a silly thought.

I approached the paintings for this book in much the same

blah indeed!

way. I set no restrictions, often working without a sketch. Working directly
on the painting kept the illustrations
as fresh as the poetry. I worked and
reworked pieces until I felt the painting had the same type of emotion as
the words it represented.

These poems are timeless. Though
some were written years ago, they still
address issues concerning today's teens.
Brutally honest and straightforward, these
are poems that we can all relate to in
many ways, but at the same time they are
uniquely personal.

—ESTHER PEARL WATSON

TRUST

The sweetness in your voice
vibrates inside my soul
as I touch you
I can feel much more than your soft skin
I can feel the pain within
You look at me like you want to speak
and then shut yourself
because you are afraid
of being wrong
everything you say
doesn't bother me
just as long as you believe
in me

Teresa Ruth, 18

THOUGHTS of THE DIFFERENT

Why? You ask why?
Why I choose to be an outsider?
Well first of all when you choose
You're not really an outsider
Second, because that's the way I am.
Crowds make me uncomfortable,
I don't like to dance
I don't like *their* groups
I don't understand *them, their* language
I don't understand *them*, and you know what?
I don't want to.
I don't want to because, I think if I did
I wouldn't be the way I am.
Happy.
And if I changed to the point where I *do* understand *them*
I think I'd die
That's all and that's why.

Adi Givati, 14

BLIND

Out of you,
And the Mirror
On the wall.
Neither of you
See me at all.
You can't tell,
If I lie,
Or if I,
Want to die.
It's the true me
You'll have to find.
Until then
You'll remain blind.

Jason Owen Douglas Hylton, 14

WASTE O' TIME

Your eyes are like stars
    —distant and shining
Your fingers cold like metal bars
    —stiffly intertwining

I look for love,
    for warmth
  of some sort.
So far,
    —I've found nothing,
  I'm sorry to report.

Strange,
    and far
  is your mind.
I feel
    for the heart
  I am trying to find.

Your stubbornness
    and my love
  shall never combine.
So honey,
    let go of me.
  —You're wasting my time.

Mary Kadzielski, 15

BLUSH

A circle of women
today includes
me.
they laugh more than
I thought they would.
they're more honest
about their
lovers
sometimes
they talk about their sex
like we're leaky faucets—
all sorts of liquids
drip down our thighs,
from our underarms and noses
(I blush)
sometimes
I wonder if this
girl,

      scared but yearning for
      these women
      this power
        this experience
is old enough
for their circles
for their wicked jokes

I wonder if they blushed too
     (I hope so.)

Emily L. Bate, 15

18

The Pain Tree

Can't you feel it?
It hurts so bad!
You can't?
What's wrong with you?
How come you can't feel it?
I don't believe you.
What do you feel?
Nothing!
No pain?
Just nothing, huh?
Well, let me tell you,
You're missin' out.
It's wonderful.

Mark Todd, 16

ZOMBIES

I don't care that so many are zombies
                    (just walking around)
Just remember the blood inside me
                                    is mine.
And although I know I shouldn't have to fight for it
                                            I will.
Even though violence doesn't
                        prove anything.
I'm not going to lie down and let some fiend
                                suck my life away.
I will be the last one
                    to be taken.
I will fight till
            the end.
Zombies—
            I can deal with
Now what about my
            "friends"?

                            Shannon Kerner, 16

Final Words

She came floating downhill on a green thought.
Searching, searching, she found the me she sought.
Her radiant lips spoke softly to me
Iambic pentameter I could see:
"I love you. I love you. I love you. Do?"
I answered in like with iambic too:
"You love me. You love me. You love me? Dread."
She lied, I sighed, nothing more need be said.

Larry D. Griffin, 16

NoT A DoLL

Why do you treat me like this
As not a girl but a toy
For your mind to play with
A doll for you to mess with
And think your perverted
Little thoughts about
I am a woman never bowing to the things you do
For I am not that way
I have my dignity and my pride
The power to believe in my image
And to stand up for my kind
To believe I am better than the way you treat me
As if I am too stupid to know
What you are doing
Too oblivious to see the way you look at me
Staring with your strange looks
And deep unblinking eyes
Things I don't understand yet too
Afraid to ask you why I wish that someday you will
See me as a lovely woman and not a doll

Carrie Ann Sirna, 13

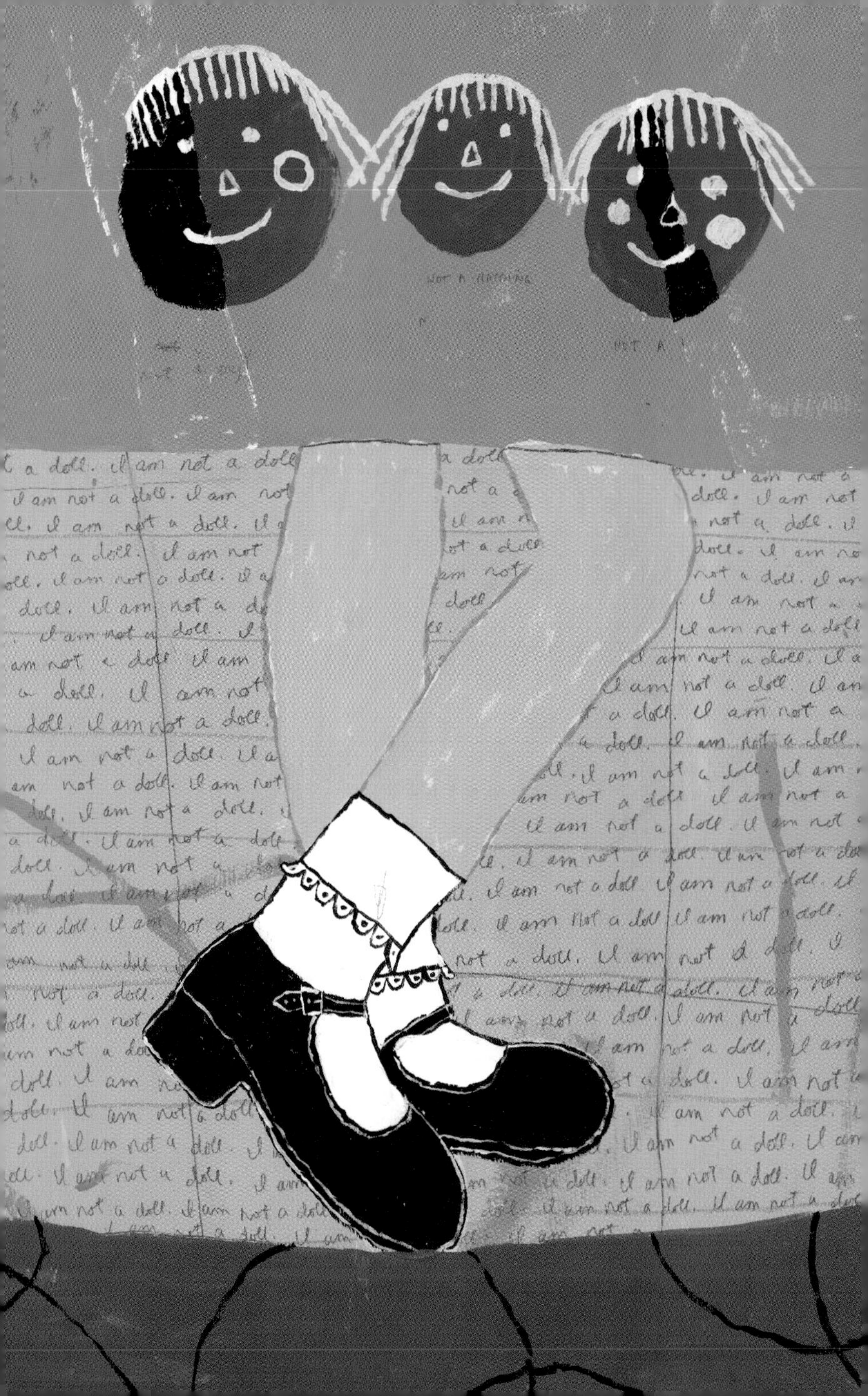
I am not a doll.

in (MY) MIND

There I stand,
Alone in the cold.
There is a storm
Constantly raging.
A tall brick wall
Stands in front of me.
On the other side,
I can hear the laughter
And see the light.
In my hand
I hold the invitation.
The door is within my reach.
But my feet won't move.
I am scared.
Will they understand who I am?
Not the act I perform around them,
But the real me?
Then I think,
Do I want them to?

Kate Engelbert, 15

CHALK

Love is like a piece of chalk
First it's brand new
Never been used
Then
With time
It fades away slowly
Until there is nothing left
But a small, tiny piece
That cannot be held anymore

Rebecca Ann Brown, 13

Nervous

I stare at you,
Hoping you'll see me
And give a smile.
Please, my sun; warm my heart.

I sob within,
Knowing you'll not come
And I'm alone.
Possibly forever.

I blink, surprised,
Fearing your approach
And its outcome.
What if you dislike me?

I freeze in place,
Entranced by your smile
And your greeting.
You're the stuff of my dreams.

I smile at you,
Glad for your presence
And your welcome.
I don't need tomorrow.

Alessandro Lopez, 15

NICE NICE NICE

Nice
Nice
Nice

Everybody's nice
Split your head twice
Beat them in the rib
Wait until it bleeds
Watch the colors run
Laugh and call it fun
Cry for all the pain
And then repeat again

Esther Pearl Watson, 15

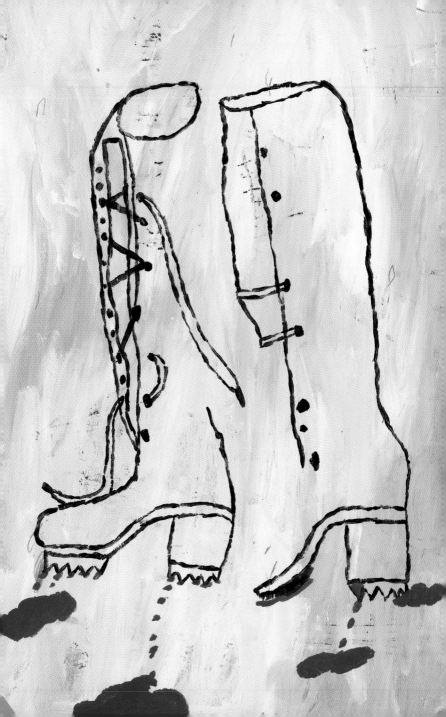

THE HAND

A seed is tenderly placed in a pot
Of dark, moist dirt which the Hand
Has prepared for it.
Nutrients lie placidly, waiting for
The time when the seed will draw
Upon them.
The seed drinks in the moisture
And struggles to break free of
Its tiny skin.
The warm sun on the moist soil
Brings about the day when the
seed triumphantly begins to
unfold, the tiny stem emerging
into the sunlight.
The Hand is delighted and waters it.
The seed is quite smug as it
Grows towards the sun.
It does not realize its need
For the sun and the Hand.
It only sees itself creating
The miracles of growth.
Will it ever learn?

Janet Hamlin, 17

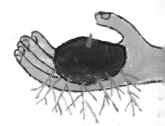

FOLLOWING DIRECTIONS

Another day of studying the Blueprints of Standard.

Another day to bind and gag **Originality.**

Another day **Free Spirit** is securely handcuffed.
   Assignments and projects are the same size, same color.
   No different from the others.

Check **Creative Thought** and **Imagination** at the entrance.

Carefully place feet in the footprints formed before.

Step through the door
   Where the thick gray **Dull** descends and surrounds to begin
   Another day of following directions.

Adam Overcash, 14

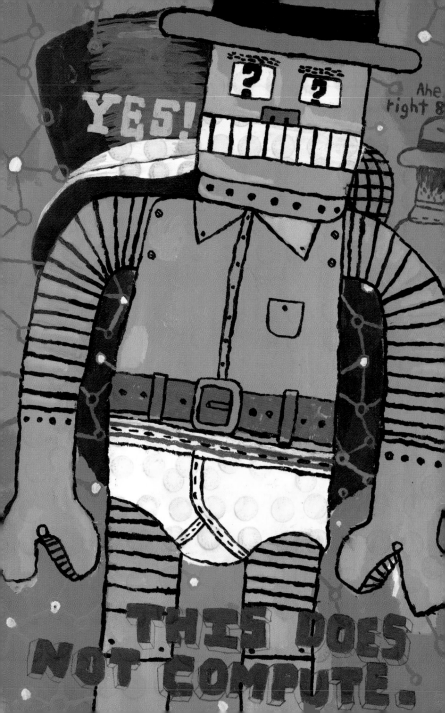

HATE

Why so controversial about someone?
Why so much hate from this?

HATE

Hate for two people who love each other,
There is nothing to hate about this,
It is just that they are the same sex,
It doesn't bother me,
But it sure as hell bothers other people,
God made us equal,
If he knew back then what he knows now about our problems with hate,
He wouldn't have bothered with woman or man kind . . .

Michelle Cuadros, 13

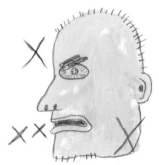

EXASPERATION

Sick is my mother
So why does no one bother?

The idiot father
Contemptuously would rather
Give out orders through his nose
Than slightest decency give to the matter.

The egotist brother
Self absorbedly would rather
Self indulgently before the computer sit
Than guilt seconds spare with dear mother.

He who (I thought) knows better (crazy indeed)
He who feels deeply (about himself)
He who shows signs of intelligence (lacking compassion)
He who abhors the jerk our father (himself no improvement) is
He who exists in a world with only himself.

Am I the only who cares to help in mom's despair?
(yet it is not much that I do)
Am I the only to see her pain and care?
Blast ye souls to hell for this.
Show your wife some respect . . .
Show your mother you're perfect . . .
No! You treat her with indifference
As you would a wilting flower.
I rage inside with anger immense,
Yet you are armed with defense.
Unfinished the battles remain—
Mother the loser again.

Paula Rzeczkowski, 17

I'm too _____ to die.
(please fill in the blank)

Peter Hamlin, 18

"Wake Up"

It's not from your sleep,
But yet from your dreams
Because you all fail to realize
Life is harder than it seems.
You see it every day
But yet you still walk away,
'Cause when it stares you in the face,
You know not what to say.

You say you want power,
But you still run like a coward.
That's like saying you hate water,
But every night taking a shower.
Stop thinking of all your worst wishes,
The things you know are corrupt.
You need to stop thinking at all,
And take the time to wake up.

David W. Moore, 15

SWEET

To kiss you was . . . Sweet.
The feel of your tongue on my teeth was
 . . . Sweet.
Your lips against mine were . . . Sweet.
The way you moved your tongue in my
mouth was . . . Sweet (and it made me
shiver).
The force of your kiss took me and it was
 . . . Sweet.
I had bruises on the inside of my mouth
for a week and it was . . . Sweet.
I was amazed by my first real kiss and it
was . . . Sweet.
I remember our lips meeting at a party,
Dane, and that was . . . Sweet.
Take all the kisses in your life and put
them on a tape. Plug yourself in. Never
push stop. Now, that would be . . . Sweet.

Mandy Foster, 17

"FRIENDLY" HIGH

I think he's the one for me,
    but then I realize the only one for him is his "bud."
He looks and says hi to me,
    but do those glazed eyes see the real me?
He jokingly punches me when he walks away,
    but he doesn't understand that when he touches me it's like a
    punch to my heart.
I think I like him so much,
    but I know he likes his "bud" more.
I know I can never replace the feeling he gets from his "bud,"
    but I think the high I'd give would be better.

Jamie Leigh Dowling, 16

The Ice Cream Vendors

(In honor of the Working Boys Center, Quito, Ecuador)

Swarming like vultures
On children at play,
The ice cream vendors
Enticingly ring melodic bells
Luring like Sirens singing to sailors long ago.
Slowly they cruise the park.

Yielding to devilish temptation,
Whimsical children hand over
Hard-earned money and bus fare home
For fleeting moments
Of ice-cold delight.
Walking away with a smile,
The ice cream vendors,
Gloat in subtle deceit,
Cocky as the snake,
That slithered off with Eden's innocence.

Meanwhile, the street children's tears of despair
Mingle with melting ice cream,
On the long trudge home.

Justin T. Meyers, 18

WHAT DID I DO?

Inspired by Rosa Parks

What did I Do?
Why can't I eat with you?
You play far away in the park
You say I'm too dark

I get abused
Black
It's not an excuse
I sit on the back of the bus
We belong with you, you belong with us

So I cry
Ask God why?
You are so mean
And
You can't see

How it feels to be me
What Did I Do?

Vinette Bartley, 13

CANDY

(Dedicated to a young woman who did not notice love)

Your passionate beauty
Your sweet perfume
Were all blessed upon you
In your mother's womb

The devil's own anger
Clenched in fists of rage
Was sealed within
Your immortal cage

For if not for hate
You would have no love
And if not for anger
You'd be peaceful as a dove

Yet you're eternally happy
For you still have one
I'll wander in misery
For I'll always have none

Michael J. Shoultz, 15

MAGGOT MEMORIES

Wake me from this dream
This horrible, horrible dream
Where art is life
And life is pain
And pain is when you scream
I walk these aisles
by myself
I'm gonna walk
myself to death
moving along
like a slug
in a world too
fast for me
Leaving a trail
of blood and glass
That slime of a past—
Dragging it all behind me. . . .

Alice Nadina, 18

THE POETS

Teresa Ruth wrote "Trust" while at Job Corps in Guthrie, Oklahoma, a youth facility that provides education and job skills for struggling teens.

Adi Givati lives in Kfar Saba, Israel, where she likes to write short stories and hopes to live on Mars when she grows up.

Jason Owen Douglas Hylton is a freshman at Righetti High School, in Santa Maria, California, "who knows there's someone different in all of us."

Mary Kadzielski lives in California and hopes not to someday.

Emily L. Bate said "Blush" was "a true experience about my aunts and mother on a family vacation."

Mark Todd wrote "The Pain Tree" in Las Vegas one afternoon after he dyed his hair black.

Shannon Kerner is currently a victim of her own creativity, aimlessly wandering the streets of New York City in search of a dream.

Larry D. Griffin, who wrote "Final Words" many years ago, reports: "Poetry that I wrote nearly twenty years ago in Oklahoma reminds me today, in Tennessee, where I am professor of English and dean of arts and sciences at Dyersburg State Community College, of how little my poetry has changed."

Carrie Ann Sirna of Parma, Ohio, who wrote "Not a Doll," hopes that this poem will reach out and actually mean something to the people she wrote it for.

Kate Engelbert of Manitowac, Wisconsin, wrote "In My Mind" "during a very complicated time in my life."

Rebecca Ann Brown of Antioch, California, writes poetry because "it's the only way for me to get out my emotions without risking getting hurt by anyone."

Alessandro Lopez is a sophomore honor student at Parsippany Hills High School, New Jersey, who dreams of becoming a computer game programmer/designer.

Esther Pearl Watson wrote her poem while working at the local video store in Garland, Texas.

Janet Hamlin wrote "The Hand" while in third-period creative writing class and very proudly received a star and a smiley face.

Adam Overcash of Lakeland, Florida, said of "Following Directions": "After a seventh-grade science project received point deductions because I had not 'followed directions,' I turned my disappointment and anger into irony by writing this poem. Writing for me has always helped alleviate dark moods, and in this case, it proved to be cathartic."

Michelle Cuadros lives in southern California.

Paula Rzeczkowski is a future med student "who can get caught up in emotional whirlpools with poetry as her best medium for releasing bottled feelings."

Peter Hamlin says of his poem "I": "It was written during my last year in high school in Enumclaw, Washington, and I guess I was a bit cynical."

David W. Moore goes to Elsik High School in Houston, Texas.

Mandy Foster of Fort Worth, Texas, wrote her poem during her "techno/new wave Gary Numan-esque period."

Jamie Leigh Dowling of Holland, Ohio, is an aspiring journalist "who finally understands that sometimes your heart makes decisions that your mind normally wouldn't."

Justin T. Meyers of Kenosha, Wisconsin, says of "The Ice Cream Vendors": "I wrote this poem during the three weeks I spent volunteering at the Working Boys' Center located in Quito, Ecuador, and founded by Father John Halligan, S.J. I was inspired after observing poverty firsthand and wrote about it. The experience has changed my life."

Vinette Bartley of Brooklyn, New York, wrote "What Did I Do?" in seventh grade at Andries Huddle Junior High School.

Michael J. Shoultz of Sioux City, Iowa, wrote "Candy" for "a young woman who did not notice love."

Alice Nadina of Dallas, Texas, says of "Maggot Memories": "I don't think I have a problem with anger, I think I have a problem with the way this world works."